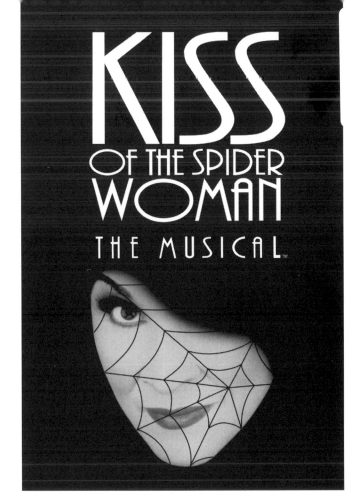

KISS OF THE SPIDER WOMAN
THE MUSICAL™

LIVENT (U.S.) Inc.
PRESENTS

Chita RIVERA
Brent CARVER   Anthony CRIVELLO
IN
KISS OF THE SPIDER WOMAN
THE MUSICAL

BOOK BY
Terrence McNALLY

MUSIC BY
John KANDER

LYRICS BY
Fred EBB

BASED ON THE NOVEL BY
Manuel PUIG

SETS & PROJECTION EFFECTS BY
Jerome SIRLIN

COSTUMES DESIGNED BY
Florence KLOTZ

LIGHTING DESIGN BY
Howell BINKLEY

SOUND DESIGN BY
Martin LEVAN

MUSICAL SUPERVISION/CONDUCTOR
Jeffrey HUARD

ORCHESTRATIONS BY
Michael GIBSON

DANCE MUSIC BY
David KRANE

ASSISTANT TO MR. PRINCE
Ruth MITCHELL

CASTING BY
JOHNSON-LIFF & ZERMAN

PRODUCTION STAGE MANAGER
Beverley RANDOLPH

CHOREOGRAPHY BY
Vincent PATERSON

ADDITIONAL CHOREOGRAPHY BY
Rob MARSHALL

DIRECTED BY
Harold PRINCE

ISBN 0-634-08476-3

EXCLUSIVELY DISTRIBUTED BY
HAL•LEONARD®
CORPORATION
7777 W. BLUEMOUND RD. P.O. BOX 13819 MILWAUKEE, WI 53213

CARLIN AMERICA

Visit Hal Leonard Online at
www.halleonard.com

VOCAL SELECTIONS

CONTENTS

ANYTHING FOR HIM

Words by Fred Ebb
Music by John Kander

SPIDER WOMAN

Soon, I feel it.

S.W.

Soon, some-how I will have him a-ny mi-nute now.

MOL   MOLINA

I'd do a-ny-thing for him he must know I'd do

6

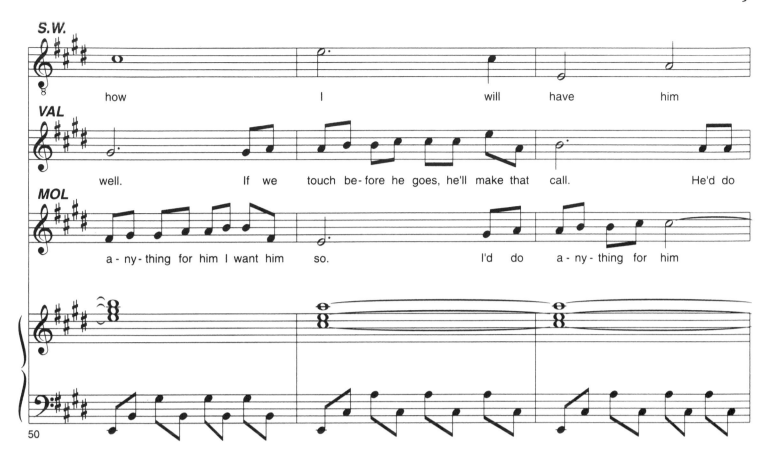

THE DAY AFTER THAT

Words by Fred Ebb
Music by John Kander

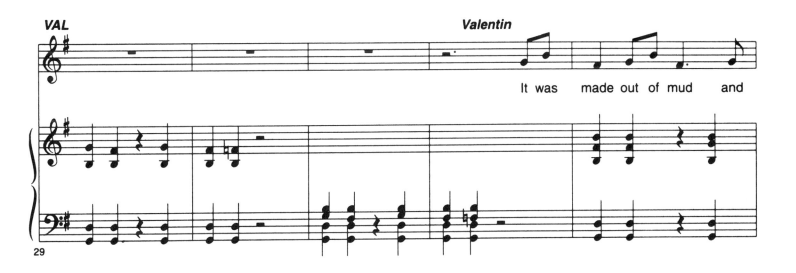

VAL

bo - xes, — my cas - tle, _____ my home.

VAL

and we slept on the floor, my sis - ter and I, with

VAL

gun - ny sacks for our pil - lows, _____ cough - ing, _____ hung - ry, _____

VAL

co - zy, _____ my home.

VAL

heard it, Thun - der rumb - ling one man

126

VAL

spea-king, thou - sands sing - ing,

rit.

Freely,

sf p

130

VAL

Some - day we'll be free. I pro - mise you we'll be free, if not to -

134

VAL

mor - row, then the day af - ter that. And the

136

DEAR ONE

Words by Fred Ebb
Music by John Kander

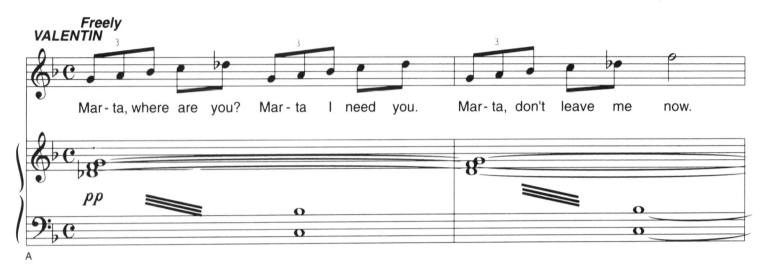

Mar-ta, where are you? Mar-ta I need you. Mar-ta, don't leave me now.

Don't let me go cra-zy.

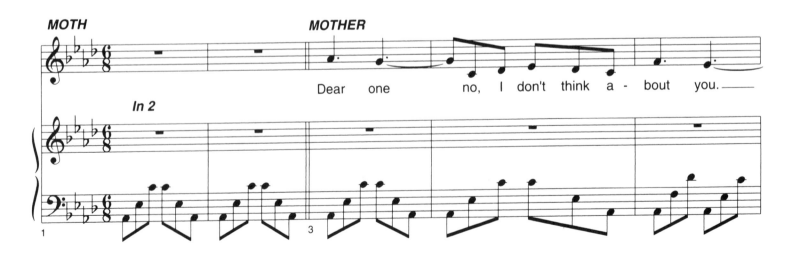

Dear one no, I don't think a-bout you.

28

DRESSING THEM UP

Words by Fred Ebb
Music by John Kander

MOL.

Ba - len - ci - a - ga it was!

65

MOL.

Dres - sing them up   I was the creme de la creme

sub p

68

MOL.

as I ad - just - ed each hem   I kept on

71

MOL.

daz - zl - ing them.   At my par - ti - cu - lar store

74

38

I DO MIRACLES

Words by Fred Ebb
Music by John Kander

AURORA

I do mi - ra-cles.

Though the lash of the whip has caused your flesh to tear,___ I will

place my lips___ on you ev' - ry - where and I'll do___

if you choose,_____ just breathe my name_____ and

there I'll be_____ do-ing mi - ra-cles._____ I do mi - ra-cles._____

_____ There are mi - ra - cles_____ in

me._____

KISS OF THE SPIDER WOMAN

Words by Fred Ebb
Music by John Kander

SPIDER WOMAN

Soon - er or la - ter you're cer - tain to meet in the bed - room, the
Soon - er or la - ter your love will ar - rive and he touch - es your

par - lor or e - ven the street. There's no place on earth you're
heart. You're a - lert and a - live and there's on - ly one pin that can

48

50

ONLY IN THE MOVIES

Words by Fred Ebb
Music by John Kander

Valentin enters

Aurora
enters

fff

MOL

Op - ti - mis - tic en - dings,_____ pas - sio- nate ro- man - ces,_____

MOL

beau - ti - ful - ly bee - fy he - roes ta - king death de - fy - ing chan - ces,_____

MOL

on - ly in the mo vies._____ De - cor- ous ma - don- nas,_____

MOL

prin - cess lay dy - ing she raised her love - ly head. And, as her lo - ver knelt be - side her,

124

MOL

very freely

this is what she said, look - ing in - to those stee - ly blue eyes of his she cried, "Vi - va la

127

MOL

guer - ra! Vi - va la re - vo - lu - ci - on!

130

Aurora stands up

MOL

Vi - va what- e-ver it is!"

133

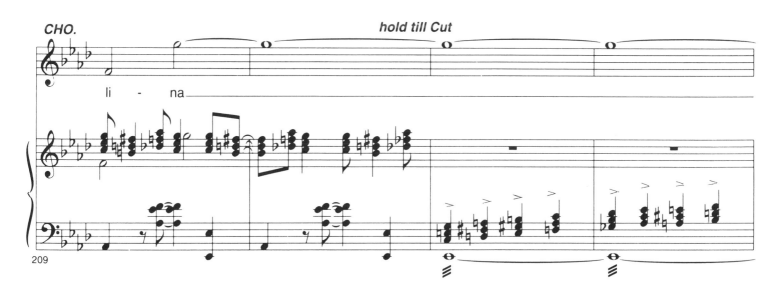

THE MORPHINE TANGO 1

Words by Fred Ebb
Music by John Kander

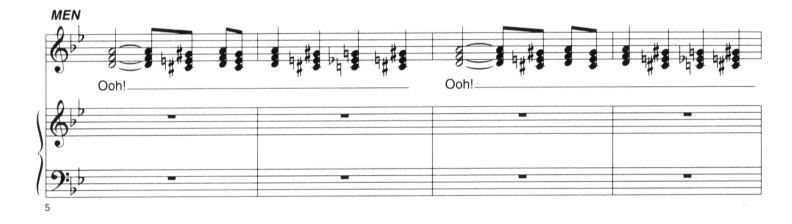

Ooh!_____ Ooh!_____

First you take your arm and stick it out. Then you take a tube you

MEN

stick   it   in.   A- ny se - cond now you'll

20

MEN

feel   no   pain___   just   ooh,   ooh,   ooh,   ooh,

23

MEN

ooh,   ooh,   ooh,   ooh!   Not

rit.

a tempo

a tempo

rit.

mp

25

MEN

bad   is

27

OVER THE WALL 2

Words by Fred Ebb
Music by John Kander

WHERE YOU ARE

Words by Fred Ebb
Music by John Kander

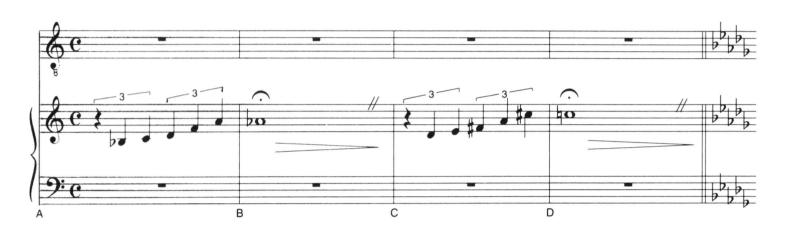

MOLINA
Rubato

When you feel you've gone to hell in a hand bas-ket And the world in which you dwell's no pa-ra-

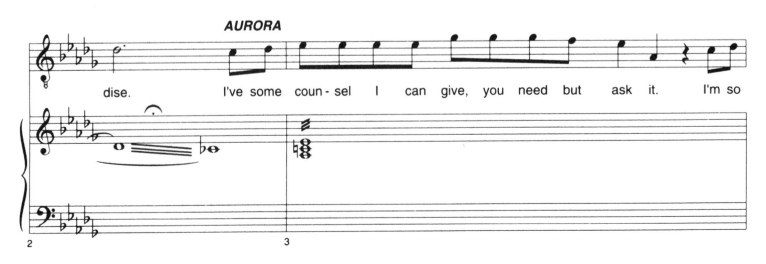

AURORA

dise. I've some coun-sel I can give, you need but ask it. I'm so

face re - a - li - ty,__ the more you scar.__ So close your

eyes and you'll be - come a movie star.__ Why

must you stay__ where you are?__

You've got to learn how not to see

what you've seen. The slice of hell you

(Light)

call your life___ is harsh and mean._____ So why not

lie be - side me on___ a mo-vie screen._____

Why must you see_____

what you've_ seen? And if you find that you land in jail,_

a lit - tle fan - ta - sy will not fail. It's just as

sim - ple as "A B C." Come up here.

Play with me.

Play with me.

AURORA & MEN

You've got to learn how not to do

If you run a - way _____ some

ma - ti - nee _____ from where you are. _____

88

Cups & Plates Banging

Samba/Rag Feel

100

103

AURORA

So why not

106

Play with me.

MEN

AURORA

You've got to learn how not to do

what you've done. The pis-tol shot can't

ma - ti - nee_____ from where you are.___

AURORA & MEN

And if you

find that you land in jail,_____ a lit-tle fan-ta-sy will not fail.__

Slower (Swing)

It's just as sim-ple as "A B C."_____

AURORA

And I can prom-ise you   you will   find___   you will

MEN

Ooh_____

194

a tempo

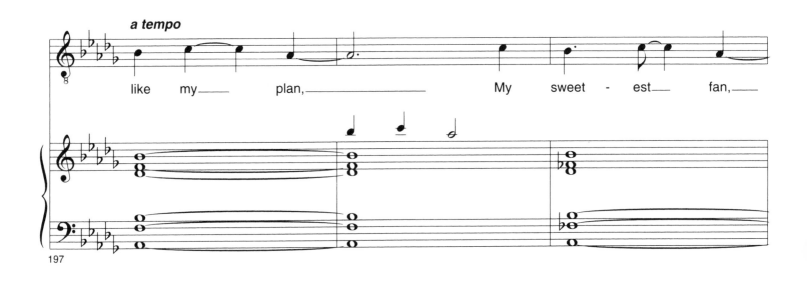

like   my___   plan,_____   My   sweet - est___   fan,___

197

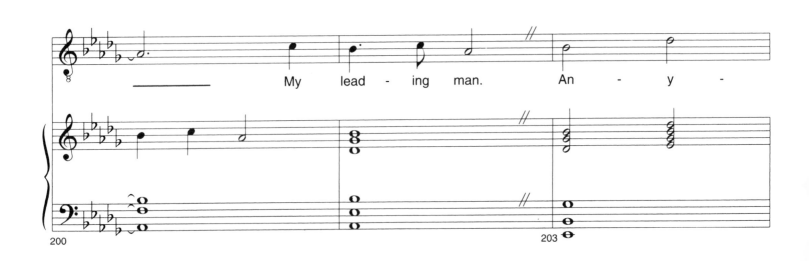

_____   My   lead - ing   man.   An - y -

200   203

where you are.

SHE'S A WOMAN

Words by Fred Ebb
Music by John Kander